THE PRACTICAL STRATEGIES SERIES
IN GIFTED EDUCATION

series editors
FRANCES A. KARNES & KRISTEN R. STEPHENS

Working With Gifted English Language Learners

Michael S. Matthews

PRUFROCK PRESS, INC.

ISBN-13: 978-1-59363-195-6
ISBN-10: 1-59363-195-2

At the time of this book's publication, all facts and figures cited are the most current available. All telephone numbers, addresses, and Web site URLs are accurate and active. All publications, organizations, Web sites, and other resources exist as described in the book, and all have been verified. The authors and Prufrock Press, Inc., make no warranty or guarantee concerning the information and materials given out by organizations or content found at Web sites, and we are not responsible for any changes that occur after this book's publication. If you find an error, please contact Prufrock Press, Inc. We strongly recommend to parents, teachers, and other adults that you monitor children's use of the Internet.

Prufrock Press, Inc.
P.O. Box 8813
Waco, Texas 76714-8813
(800) 998-2208
Fax (800) 240-0333
http://www.prufrock.com

Contents

The Practical Strategies Series in Gifted Education offers teachers, counselors, administrators, parents, and other interested parties up-to-date instructional techniques and information on a variety of issues pertinent to the field of gifted education. Each guide addresses a focused topic and is written by scholars with authority on the issue. Several guides have been published. Among the titles are:

- *Acceleration Strategies for Teaching Gifted Learners*
- *Curriculum Compacting: An Easy Start to Differentiating for High-Potential Students*
- *Enrichment Opportunities for Gifted Learners*
- *Independent Study for Gifted Learners*
- *Motivating Gifted Students*
- *Questioning Strategies for Teaching the Gifted*
- *Social & Emotional Teaching Strategies*
- *Using Media & Technology With Gifted Learners*

For a current listing of available guides within the series, please contact Prufrock Press at (800) 998-2208 or visit http://www.prufrock.com.

Rapidly changing demographics are not a new phenomenon in the history of the United States. Throughout our nation's history, there have been cyclic increases and decreases in immigration rates (Noel, 2000). These cycles ebb and flow on a scale measured in decades, and to the casual observer watching, they may not appear cyclical at all. Because our lives are short compared to the scale of change, the rapid increases in immigration observed since the early 1990s seem like a new phenomenon to many people, whose ancestors themselves arrived in the U.S. only a few generations ago. Something is indeed different in recent years, but it is less obvious than the arrival of immigrants themselves; it is the goals of our educational system.

Prior to recent decades, and particularly before World War II, relatively few Americans attended college. After the war, the GI Bill provided financial assistance that allowed many more people to further their education. Since that time, changes in the types of jobs available and competition for well-paying positions have made pursuing a college degree more of a necessity for all than a luxury for the privileged few. Most parents today would like their children to attend college. For public schools, too, a major goal has become to prepare all students for college. This, then, is the fundamental difference between our educational efforts today and those of yesteryear. In earlier times, it was assumed that only a few select students would attend college. Today, our educational system strives to educate all students for postsecondary education, regardless of their origins, home language, or economic status.

Most recently, the No Child Left Behind Act of 2001 (NCLB) has given the goal of educating all students the force of law. Schools now face sanctions or other harsh consequences if any demographic group of students fails to make adequate yearly progress (AYP). Adequate yearly progress is defined based on scores on standardized tests. These scores must go up each year, toward the goal of all students scoring at predetermined high levels, for a school to meet its AYP goals. Students who are learning English as an additional language are one of the groups having the greatest difficulty under these new legislative requirements (Abedi, 2004; Sternberg, 2004; Wright, 2005).

Allowing capable students the opportunity to receive an appropriate education should require little thought or debate. Those students who are able to learn more rapidly and in greater depth and complexity than their peers must be given every opportunity to do so. Providing students with appropriate educational experiences should be schools' primary goal, and gifted education programs exist to serve the needs of highly able students just as other forms of special education address the individual needs of students who differ from their "average" peers in other ways. Gifted programs generally are not mandated like other areas of special education. Even when gifted programs do exist, many students who would benefit from them are never given the opportunity to participate.

English Language Learners (ELL) are poorly represented in gifted programs, for a variety of reasons (Castellano, 2003; Castellano & Díaz, 2002). In particular, language differences may prevent these students from scoring high on standardized tests, in large part because these tests are administered almost entirely in English. In addition to lower test scores, the individuals who make decisions in schools may wrongly believe that only students proficient in English can be gifted (Aguirre, 2003). Finally, cultural preferences may lower a child's willingness to be singled out for academic prowess, causing the otherwise qualified child (or, more importantly, his or her parents) to decline to participate in a school's gifted program.

Despite these and other barriers, schools bear the responsibility for providing all students with an appropriate education. In particular, the 1975 Public Law 94–142 (more recently renamed the Individuals with Disabilities Education Act or IDEA) stipulated that each school-age child is to be provided "a free, appropriate public education" regardless of his or her disability. Although laws do not mandate services for academically gifted children, most states now offer at least minimal services for gifted students, as well. Research has clearly portrayed the negative consequences of failing to challenge gifted children, particularly underachievement and dropping out of school (Matthews, in press; Renzulli & Park, 2002; Rimm & Lovance, 1992). Thus, highly able students who fail to receive appropriate educational services may not do well in school, an outcome that is not always envisioned.

Gifted students do benefit from receiving an appropriate education that takes their academic and social needs into account. This is the major principle underlying the provision of gifted education, though it has not always been communicated effectively to those outside the field. However, this is not the only benefit such programs provide. Other students also benefit when their peers achieve academically; for example, research has shown that students in the regular classroom learn more quickly when their peers are of higher academic ability (Betts, Zau, & Rice, 2003). Therefore, more effectively meeting the needs of gifted ELL students through appropriate programming would benefit everyone involved. Not only does providing educational enrichment to qualified ELL students meet their educational needs, but it also may help to raise the average test scores of this group of students, and thereby help satisfy the AYP requirements that schools are now required to meet.

This guide provides teachers with an introduction to working with English Language Learners, with an emphasis on how these practices may affect the identification and education of gifted ELL students. Such information will not only raise teachers' consciousness on an important educational issue, but will also benefit those students whose potential contributions to the classroom and the world may not be realized if schools fail to meet their educational needs.

Although many of the examples and resources in this publication focus on Spanish-speaking ELL students, the process of second language learning is quite similar no matter what languages are involved. The language learning process depends on being human, not on membership in any particular linguistic or cultural group. Therefore, the processes and general approaches described here may be used with any students who are learning English.

Readers with extensive experience in education have probably noticed that the labels commonly used to refer to particular groups have changed over the years, as society has become more aware of the impact such labels may have on students. In the case of students whose first language is not English, one early label was Limited English Proficient. This label is no longer favored because it is considered a "deficit" view, focusing on what students cannot do, rather than on what they can do. More generally, it also suggests that English is always more important than other languages a student may know.

Other labels, including English as a Second Language (ESL) and English to Speakers of Other Languages (ESOL), are still in use, but are more appropriately used to describe a particular type of program or educational approach, rather than used as a label for the students who are participating in these programs. Likewise, Bilingual Education also describes a particular type of program, rather than a characteristic of students served by such a program. The label for students that is currently most favored is English Language Learner (ELL). This term is descriptive, yet it implies no value judgment about the students it describes. It also allows for more latitude than ESL, as it does not presume English to be the student's second language when it may in fact be the third or fourth language a student is learning.

The majority of ELL students in the United States speak Spanish or Vietnamese at home. These students are often first-generation immigrants to the United States, but they most commonly are born in the U.S. to immigrant parents (Klein, Burgarin, Beltranena, & McArthur, 2004). In some locales, such as the American Southwest or parts of California, families may have resided in the United States for many generations, yet not speak English at home. This may also hold true for Native American students. The number of ELL students has grown dramatically in recent years, which helps explain the increase in interest expressed about meeting these students' educational needs.

English Language Learners may have parents who are professionals, refugees, or are students in the United States attending graduate school. Home languages may include Haitian Creole, Hmong, or any of the thousands of languages spoken around the world. Thus, each school and classroom will have a different mix of students. The key to working successfully with children is to have an awareness of both their individuality and the characteristics they share with other children of similar age.

Before discussing how to find gifted English Language Learners, or how to meet their needs, it is helpful to have a context in which to place this new information. A brief introduction to language and culture follows to help readers having different levels of familiarity reach a shared understanding of these important issues.

What Is Language?

The word *language* is used in many different ways, from the language of bees to the languages of ASCII (computer code) and even the Klingon language from *Star Trek*. What these varied usages share is the notion of communication, as language is a shared system of communication.

Language is not the same as speech. Speech is making sounds; language is the meaning conveyed by the sounds. American Sign Language is a well-developed system of communication, demonstrating that language can exist even without speech. Language conveys meaning through symbols, which often have no obvious connection to the things they represent. Thus, language must be shared among a community of users for the symbols to have a culturally accepted meaning.

Another trait makes human language nearly unique—it is primarily a learned behavior. This means that a human infant eventually can learn to speak perfectly in any language to which he or she is exposed. Because language is learned, it is also exceptionally flexible. New words can be invented as needed, or old ones modified to take on new meanings. Many words that we presently use every day did not exist 10, 20, or 50 years ago. Flexibility is an important factor in the language learning process, especially for academically gifted students (Aguirre, 2003), as will be explained later.

Language Versus Dialect

There have been tens of thousands of languages spoken over the course of human history. Presently there are between 5,000 and 7,000 languages spoken in the world, depending on how they are counted. Hundreds, if not thousands, of these languages are considered endangered. It is likely that within one or two generations, as older speakers die and younger generations no longer use their traditional languages, many languages will die out (Gibbs, 2002; Skutnabb-Kangas, 2000).

There is some overlap between the concepts of *language* and *dialect*. The traditional distinction suggests that if two speakers can understand each other, they are speaking different dialects rather than different languages. Another way to state this definition is that dialects are language varieties that are mutually intelligible. It follows that American and British English, for example, or versions of American English spoken in Texas or Boston, may be considered dialects. However, Catalonian and Spanish, although quite similar in some respects, are regarded as separate languages. The different spoken varieties of Chinese, although mostly unintelligible, are linked by a common written language and therefore are usually referred to as dialects.

Another somewhat more fanciful definition, of uncertain origin although widely quoted, quips, "A language is a dialect with an army." This definition can be invoked to explain why Danish and Norwegian are considered separate languages, even though for the most part they are mutually understood. Thus, although there is some overlap, different dialects are generally more similar to one another than different languages are.

Dialects carry practical implications for the classroom setting. As is the case with languages, particular dialects can confer higher or lower prestige on their speakers in different settings. The classroom setting tends to favor those students who share the teacher's dialect, which in the United States is usually (but not always) standard American English.

An important implication of dialectical differences is that these may provide an audible indicator that suggests to the alert teacher the possibility of other, less readily observable cultural differences. In other words, subtle dialectical differences may help the teacher be sensitive to the presence of other cultural differences that can influence students' classroom behaviors. This possibility leads us to a brief consideration of culture.

What Is Culture? Whose Culture Is Valuable?

As mentioned previously, language is shared across a community of users, and it is this shared contextual usage that gives a particular set of otherwise-arbitrary language symbols their meaning. Language forms a part of culture. Culture may be defined quite broadly from the perspectives of anthropology and linguistics as a shared set of meanings and behaviors that are reproduced among a group of individuals. Although some ongoing disagreements remain, this broad definition is sufficient for a basic understanding of classroom interaction.

Race and ethnicity are quite visible, even more so than economic class or language, and therefore they offer a readily available basis on which people can form groups. Broader differences in language and culture tend to occur along racial or ethnic lines as well, lending strength to these groupings. The human mind is also quite adept at forming stereotypes, which are categories of people or things that share similar traits. This ability exists for good reason, as we would be overwhelmed without it. But, the drawback to these tendencies is that they work together to predispose us to group and judge others almost instantly, yet not always accurately.

Stereotyping, even when it occurs unconsciously, can therefore lead to fewer nonmainstream children being included in gifted programs or other academically advanced classes. Aguirre (2003) offers some examples that illustrate how students' academic abilities might be misperceived in this manner. Mainstream culture, she notes, "values cooperation, independence, and initiative" (p. 19). Students from different cultures often hold different values in one or more of these areas, and these differences can hinder these students' performance in the classroom.

Multiculturalism in the Classroom

The vast majority of teachers are White, female, and middle class. In most classroom settings, at least some of the students with whom these teachers interact are non-White. Because of the potential ill effects of stereotyping based on linguistic and cultural differences, teachers need to make a conscious effort to become aware of their own perceptions and to monitor their own thought processes in order to be confident that they are treating all of their students equitably. Multiculturalism offers a theoretical framework within which to make these efforts.

Several theories have been developed to consider the relative social positions of different groups in our society (Howard, 1999). Analysis of these consistently shows that privileges accrue to the dominant social group (Whites, in most of the U.S.), whether or not group members are consciously aware of it (Noel, 2000). Also, Whites in the United States tend to believe that they have no culture (Howard; Noel), although anthropological, educational, and psychological studies demonstrate otherwise. It is quite difficult to step back from one's own cultural surroundings to examine them, although several researchers have provided accessible accounts of their personal observations, as well as the implications of such examination for classroom instruction (Banks, 1995; Ford & Harris, 1999; Ford, Moore, & Milner, 2005; Gay, 2000; Howard; Noel; Torrance, Goff, & Satterfield, 1998).

Banks (1995) suggested several important characteristics that effective multicultural education programs should have. At the classroom level, these characteristics include teaching using nonstereotypical examples depicting individuals from diverse groups; helping students develop positive attitudes and behaviors toward other groups; and consciously examining and modifying teaching strategies to provide equal educational opportunities to students from all cultural and racial groups, as well as to students from different social classes. At the school level, the environment should offer equal status within the culture of the school to students from diverse groups. Such efforts at providing equivalent status to two languages are particularly visible in the context of dual-language school programs.

These suggestions sound straightforward, yet are difficult to achieve in practice. An ongoing commitment to personal and professional development is required, and maintaining this commitment takes hard work. Fortunately, teachers tend to be highly dedicated to their profession, and increasing numbers of educators are willing to make these efforts.

How do the preceding paragraphs relate to the educational needs of highly able students? There are multiple connections. Aguirre (2003) emphasizes the importance of valuing students' home language and culture. She notes that myths about linguistically different gifted students abound, as in the belief that these students "are different and will have to acculturate before they can understand aspects of giftedness valued by the dominant culture" (p. 18). Clearly, the teacher who has come to a personal understanding of multicultural issues will recognize the fallacy in this statement, and will be able to assist the nonmainstream student in reaching a similar understanding.

It should be noted that some observers have found tension between the values of multicultural education and those of gifted education. "After all," their argument goes, "how can we offer equal opportunities to all our students when we are giving extra opportunities to this one group?" Readers may encounter this argument themselves some day, and may wonder how to respond. As VanTassel-Baska (2003) has argued, this point of view undervalues intellectual diversity in comparison with diversity in other cultural and performance areas. Most schools would never try to include every student on their basketball team, nor would they select soloists at random for the school band. Rather, students demonstrate their abilities and are offered specialized instruction when it is needed. As VanTassel-Baska notes, "if we are serious about promoting diversity, then support for individual differences of all types should be the norm in schools and classrooms, not the exception" (p. 2).

What does it mean to say that someone "knows a language"? Everyone probably has some intuitive idea of how to answer this question, and the common element in these answers would likely involve the ability to communicate. Communication is indeed the heart of language, but this is like saying that salty water is the ocean; there is quite a bit more about languages and oceans worth describing. Teachers working with students who speak different languages will want to know a bit more background information about language learning. Below are some common misconceptions about language learning, followed by a discussion of first and second language learning.

Common Misconceptions About Language Learning

Adults who are unfamiliar with the research in this field often have many misconceptions about language learning that can lead to inappropriate educational decisions. Below are several common misconceptions in this area, drawn primarily from Baker's (2000; 2001) work.

- *Learning a second language interferes with development of the first language.*
  False: There is more than enough room in the brain for two or more languages. Additional languages build upon and are integrated with the child's first language, expanding his or her verbal abilities rather than stunting them.

- *Students should only learn English because it is the majority language in the United States.*
  False: The mind does not "fill up" with one complete language; rather, skills developed in another language can help students learn English. Denying students the opportunity to maintain their linguistic heritage can create a loss of identity, disrupting students' relations with family and friends, and possibly lowering their academic achievement. Maintaining bilingualism actually can improve students' job prospects, as many employers are seeking workers who can communicate effectively in more than one language.

- *Mixing languages shows a lack of competence in either language.*
  False: Language mixing following grammatical rules is called code switching, and is a purposeful communication strategy used to convey added meaning. Except in rare cases involving language disorders, code switching is a normal characteristic of speakers using two or more languages.

- *People may make fun of children who speak another language in public.*
  True: But, it is usually people who speak only one language who engage in this sort of behavior, and it is only one of many ways minorities may be made to feel unwelcome in mainstream society (Howard, 1999; Noel, 2000). This is not a sufficient reason to give up being bilingual. Building children's self-esteem, based on their abilities, is important in helping them deal effectively with the prejudices of others.

- *Children should learn to read in English before they learn another language.*
  Depends. Children most commonly learn to read in one language before the other, although some children learn in both simultaneously. Children first should be taught to read in their stronger language. Their literacy skills will transfer readily to those in the weaker language, and their progress will be faster.

- *Children can only learn a second language well when they are very young.*
  Mostly True. Children more easily develop native pronunciation in a second language when they learn it before age 7. Between the ages of 7–12, such learning or acquisition becomes more difficult, in part because of the increasing cognitive demands of the school curriculum during these years. By the ages of 13 and older, when many schools offer a foreign language class for the first time, it is quite difficult for students to become as proficient in a new language as a native speaker. This is why it is important for schools to support students' bilingual abilities from an early age.

- *Teachers must speak the child's home language to be effective working with ELL students.*
  False. It is helpful if teachers who work with ELL students have learned some language other than English themselves, for it helps them empathize with what their students are going through in learning English. Knowledge of another language also helps make teachers more aware of the language acquisition process, of the structural and grammatical differences between English and other languages, and of the sheer complexity of the language learning process. It can also be a tremendous help in communicating with parents. However, students in schools in the United States may speak any number of different languages, sometimes all within a single school, and it is rare for even the most qual-

ified teaching staff to know more than a handful of these. It may also be perceived as unfair if a teacher appears to be providing more help to those students who speak a second language that he or she also speaks. Therefore, while it certainly can be helpful if a teacher knows the child's home language, it is by no means necessary.

Learning a First Language

Every child learns almost automatically the language spoken in his or her environment. It does not seem to matter how difficult this language may be, or what sounds, if any, are necessary to speak it. One may wonder, why do we need to teach children about language if they will learn it anyway? The answer is that written language depends on oral language, and both are essential to ensure a child's success in school. Academic language includes additional components beyond social language, and academic language skills are a large part of what we teach children (Baker & Hornberger, 2001; Cummins, 1999).

Language can be broken down into several levels, thereby making this large and complex topic much easier to study. These levels include five components:

1. phonology—how sounds are put together to form larger units, such as morphemes and words;
2. morphology—the meaningful parts or units that are put together to make words;
3. syntax—how words are put together to form sentences;
4. semantics—how the meaning of sentences is determined from the words' meanings and how they are combined; and
5. discourse structure—how sentences are put together into larger units of meaning such as paragraphs.

Using these five levels, any human language can be described and compared to other languages, even though each language represents a unique pattern of rules, sounds, and meanings across these levels. Because language acquisition is an extremely complex phenomenon, only a sparse outline of this topic is presented here. For further study consult the many texts that have been written on this topic (Baker, 2000; 2001; Gonzalez, 1999; Lessow-Hurley, 2003; Piper, 2003; Tokuhama-Espinosa, 2001; Valdés, 2003).

During their first year of life, children are aware of language and they respond to it, but are not yet capable of producing it themselves. By age 2, the typical child begins to communicate intentionally with words and gestures, and can connect words to the objects they represent. Babies move from babbling sounds, to single- and then two-word utterances. Once children have learned anywhere from a few to several dozen words, their vocabulary increases rapidly and their sentences grow longer and more complex. By age 4, the typical child can produce well-formed sentences for a variety of purposes including questioning, ordering, and negating. Note that these milestones are based on observations of monolingual children. Children who are raised bilingual from birth may reach these points slightly later, although they almost always catch up with monolingual children by age 5.

By age 5 or 6, typical children have mastered most of the syntax and phonology of their primary language. They know somewhere between 2,500 and 8,000 words, depending on the child and on how the words are counted, and they can understand many more words than they can speak. Individuals will spend the next dozen or more years adding immense stores of vocabulary, mastering the subtleties of meaning and intonation, and developing reading and related literacy skills. The rate and degree to which these skills develop depends in large part upon the education the child receives, both at home and in school.

Learning a Second Language

Although it may be difficult to believe, particularly for those who are used to thinking of the United States as a leader in education, most of the children elsewhere in the world will learn more than one language before the end of their schooling (Piper, 2003). This is not the experience of many students in the United States, where opposition to bilingualism and bilingual education has been well-organized and quite vocal (Dicker, 2000). Tellingly, this opposition has not targeted mainstream programs for students who learn a foreign language for travel or business purposes, but has attacked only those programs that teach immigrants. It would seem that despite their rhetoric, these organizations are not opposed to bilingualism as such, but rather are a thinly disguised means through which to attack the right of immigrant students to receive an appropriate education (Dicker).

Second language learning is in many ways quite similar to the process of learning a first language. However, it is also more complicated, because there are many more variables involved. A second language learner may be any age; may be learning a language that is quite similar to, or quite different from, his or her first language; and may be learning the second language under any of a wide variety of environmental and social conditions. Each of these circumstances can strongly affect the rate and degree of language learning that takes place.

These variables can be narrowed somewhat by limiting the discussion to school age children living in the United States and to children who are learning English as opposed to other second languages. Applying these limitations, ELL students can be grouped into three broad categories:
- children who are only learning English at school,
- bilingual children who have learned or are learning English at home, and
- older students who are recent arrivals to U.S. schools.

The first group is made up of young children who are immigrants, or born to immigrant parents, and who are learning English in school, but not necessarily at home. These children may come to school with little or no knowledge of English, or they may be just beginning to learn the language through friends and English-language media. Their parents may both speak the same language, or two different languages, at home, so English in fact may be the child's third language. The language development of children in this group will require a large degree of well-organized support, especially in the early school years, in comparison to children who already are learning English at home. Advanced ability likely will be difficult to diagnose within this group, as these young children may have no prior school records to examine. Teacher observations and parent or peer nominations therefore may offer the most effective means of diagnosing high potential among students who are beginning to learn English in school.

The second group consists of young bilingual children who have learned or are learning English in the home, along with another language. Teachers and other adults often express concern that bilingualism may somehow be harmful to the development of English language skills, but these fears are unfounded (Baker, 2000). Evidence suggests that children raised bilingual from birth learn the two codes simultaneously, although the brain appears to process them as subsets of a single language. There is some evidence suggesting that bilingualism may lead to greater cognitive flexibility for children who are relatively fluent in more than one language (Bialystok, 1991; Martorell, 2000; Matthews, 2002b). Tests of creative ability or of vocabulary may be useful in diagnosing advanced ability within this population. Such measures should be designed to accept answers in either language, because these students, like students from the first group, are quite likely to have developed a pattern of strengths and weaknesses in each language. For example, a study of bilingual second graders found that most were unable to name geometric shapes in their first language, although they did know them in English (Matthews, 2002a). Teachers must be sensitive to these variations, and should not assume that high or low English language performance in one subject will predict language performance in a different area.

Older children who are recent immigrants present a different set of concerns. In addition to language issues, these students may have had less, or more, formal education than children their age who have attended school in the United States. Even students who have had grade-appropriate schooling may have covered concepts in a different order or with different emphases, compared with their U.S. peers. For the teacher, diagnosing and prescribing appropriate instruction for these students can be quite difficult because of these variations. Dropout rates vary with ethnicity, but tend to be high for this group for economic, as well as educational reasons, though some students in this situation also tend to become exceptional achievers (Schmid, 2001). Although the fact may seem counterintuitive, first-generation immigrants tend to have higher academic achievement than subsequent generations (Valenzuela, 1999).

For children who were advanced in math in their home country, math tests in English may or may not accurately measure their actual mathematical abilities. Advanced verbal ability is even more difficult to diagnose through testing, although it may be reflected in a faster or more in-depth acquisition of English in comparison with peers. Heritage language instruction, in which students who speak a common language at home are grouped for advanced differentiated foreign language instruction in the home language, offers one promising approach to language learning and gifted identification for students in this situation (Matthews & Matthews, 2004).

Initially, the most difficult aspect of offering gifted education to English Language Learners is determining which students can benefit from this type of instruction. In some cases, the nature of the gifted education program (e.g., programs that offer acceleration within the general curriculum) may determine the type of services that will be available for the students identified. It should be obvious that students gifted in math and identified by their high performance on a math test should not be placed in a gifted program in English or social studies, but anecdotal evidence suggests that this happens all the time. Be sure that your school has a match between its identification process and the services that students will receive once they have been identified (Granada, 2003).

Another question to consider is whether your school's program depends on having one particular teacher, and if so, what might happen if this teacher should unexpectedly depart. Ideally, gifted programs would continue regardless of the teacher in charge; but in practice, the training and skills that are needed to run a successful gifted program cannot always be replaced. Every year gifted curricula become more available, yet many gifted programs do not take advantage of these materials. Many gifted programs are quite small, and often schools have only one teacher who works with gifted students. Schools perhaps are reluctant to spend money on materials when the common, yet erroneous, belief is that gifted students will be successful without any special effort by teachers or schools (Aguirre, 2003).

Finally, gifted education regulations vary widely from one state to the next, so making general statements is difficult. Currently, most regulations rely either on intelligence test scores alone, or on multiple criteria that may include evidence of creativity, motivation, leadership, or achievement. Knowing a state's rules and regulations will serve as a guide for the effective use of the information in the following segments.

Gifted program teachers or coordinators at the school or district level are an excellent source of information, and most state departments of education and state gifted associations also describe the relevant legislation on their Web sites. There is also an up-to-date list of states' gifted education policies available online at http://www.geniusdenied.com/statepolicy.aspx. Readers should consult these sources briefly either before or just after reading the following sections, to determine which aspects of this information are most relevant to their particular situation.

Some General Principles

Testing, whether for intelligence (also called aptitude or potential) or achievement (knowledge and the ability to apply it to solve problems), has a couple of important drawbacks when it comes to identifying gifted English Language Learners. First, when testing ELL students in English, one can never be certain how much of the resulting test score reflects English proficiency and how much reflects the actual ability or knowledge the test is attempting to measure. Teachers are intelligent people, but how much of your intelligence would be reflected by your score on an IQ test given in Swahili?

Secondly, ELL students are often members of minority groups and are of low socioeconomic status. It is well-known that both ethnicity and economic status are correlated with differences in test scores at the group level on nearly every test ever written for use with children. These group differences often fall between one half and two standard deviations in magnitude, while gifted program entry historically has required scores two standard deviations or more above the overall mean. Intelligence tests are scaled to a standard deviation of either 15 or 16 points, with an average score set to equal 100, which means that ethnicity alone explains an average difference between 8 and 30 points on the scale used by most IQ tests. IQ scores for Asian students typically fall above the overall average of 100. Scores of Hispanic and Black students average lower to much lower than those of White students. These differences are quite persistent, remaining even when all potentially biased test questions have been removed or corrected. Although the causes of such differences remain a topic of intense debate, the fact remains that they do exist (Freedle, 2002; Lohman, 2005a; Naglieri & Ford, 2005; Sternberg, Grigorenko, & Bundy, 2001). Several alternative approaches have been applied to the identification of diverse gifted students, each attempting to avoid the biases of standardized tests.

The late Dr. Mary Frasier (1989), an authority on identifying gifted students from diverse backgrounds, compiled a list of best practices in identifying gifted students from diverse groups:

- The goal should be inclusion, rather than exclusion, of students.
- Data should be gathered from multiple sources; a single criterion of giftedness should be avoided.
- Both objective and subjective data should be collected.
- Professionals and nonprofessionals who represent various areas of expertise and who are knowledgeable about behavioral indicators of giftedness should be involved.
- Identification of giftedness should occur as early as possible, should consist of a series of steps, and should be ongoing.

- Special attention should be given to the different ways in which children from different cultures manifest behavioral indicators of giftedness.
- Decision making should be delayed until all relevant data on a student have been reviewed.
- Data collected during the identification process should be used in determining curriculum. (p. 214)

These recommendations provide a general sense of the characteristics that a program to effectively identify gifted English Language Learners should possess.

Language Background

At the beginning of the gifted identification process, it is advised that one learn as much as possible about the language background of students. This will help determine what language to use in the assessment process. Do not make any unfounded assumptions. Students who speak one language at school actually may speak another at home (Matthews, 2002a). Knowing a child's linguistic background will also give the teacher a more detailed understanding of his or her social background and personal history, often leading to stronger relationships between home and school.

Teachers can simply ask students about the languages they speak, and who they speak them with, but it is better to have a formal record of such information. This not only makes it easier to repeat the process later, but it also helps demonstrate that all students have been treated equitably. Appendix A is a sample of a language background survey that was developed in the course of research with Mexican American second graders. For younger students, teachers may also be able to take advantage of the home language surveys that federal guidelines require all schools to administer to students upon entry. Generic and system-specific home language survey forms are widely available online; for an example, visit: http://www.helpforschools.com/ELLKBase/forms/HomeLanguageSurveys.shtml.

It is also possible to develop a more test-like measure to directly investigate what students know in each language. Such a measure for young students might include low-level tasks such as naming objects in each language (Matthews, 2002a). This works best if all the students have the same home language, and if it is one the teacher or test administrator can speak with some fluency. The background survey as presented in Appendix A is both easier to administer and less sensitive to the particular languages involved.

Teacher Observation

Teachers know their students well, and probably have a good feel for the interests and ability level of each child in their classroom. Teachers can be an excellent source of ideas about which students might benefit from gifted program participation, but there are some potential pitfalls that need to be avoided or addressed prior to using teacher observations.

Research has shown that teacher identification of gifted students is not always accurate. In particular, nominations by teachers who do not have training in gifted education tend to be subject to particular types of bias (Siegle, 2001). Teachers tend to identify students whose behaviors do not match gender stereotypes or who have unusual interests for their age, while they tend not to identify children who are culturally different or from impoverished family backgrounds. This bias can automatically exclude most English Language Learners.

In some cases, teachers may be fearful of the consequences of labeling their students "gifted." This fear may arise when teachers are not confident about their own abilities, about the abilities of their students, or about those of the gifted program teacher. Teachers also tend to focus on students' weaknesses rather than on their strengths. If a teacher does not provide students with adequate challenges in class, some young students who have already mastered the grade-level curriculum will not be identified because the teacher is not aware of their true potential.

Aguirre (2003) lists 16 characteristics exhibited by linguistically and culturally diverse students. These are in some respects similar to the characteristics listed in the rating scale that is described in the following section. The Aguirre list also includes an eagerness to translate and an ability to understand jokes and puns related to cultural and language differences; an eagerness to share his or her native culture; and the flexibility to enable effective functioning in multiple cultural contexts. Consulting these and similar lists is one effective way teachers can familiarize themselves with the various ways giftedness may be expressed in diverse students.

In sum, professional development in recognizing gifted students is recommended if teachers are to be the primary means of finding gifted students. Such training may be available through in-service programs at the local level, through regional conferences, or via collaborative research involving university personnel. Some districts may also have personnel on staff that can offer instruction in this area.

Behavior Checklists or Rating Scales

Behavior checklists or rating scales offer one approach designed to minimize errors in the teacher nomination process. At their most basic level, these scales present a list of characteristic behaviors shown by gifted children, and teachers identify the students in their classrooms who have demonstrated these behaviors in class. Research suggests that simply asking teachers to name students who demonstrate particular characteristics, either with or without the use of a class roster, is less effective than asking teachers to rate each student individually using a point-based scale (Ashman & Vukelich, 1983).

Unfortunately, rating each student can be a time-consuming process. One very popular behavior rating instrument, the Scales for Rating the Behavioral Characteristics of Superior Students (SRBCSS; Renzulli et al., 2002), may take as long as 30 minutes per student to complete. On the positive side, the latest edition of this work now includes teacher-training exercises to help ensure that the scales are completed accurately.

As an additional advantage, behavior checklists and rating scales may also be used to collect behavioral information from parents or community members. Similar cautions apply as when teachers complete rating scales, with the added caveat that some parents may exaggerate ratings of their own children. One recently developed scale, the Clinical Assessment of Behavior, includes items designed to crosscheck for veracity to address this potential problem (Bracken & Brown, 2004). These may include several similar questions, which are phrased so that similar responses occupy opposite positions on the answer scale. For example, a truthful response to "this student can concentrate deeply on work that interests him or her" might be "strongly agree," while a truthful reply about the same student to the statement "this student is easily distracted even when working on something that interests him or her" would require the respondent to mark "strongly disagree." By incorporating several question pairs similar to these, although generally more subtle, it is possible to determine how internally consistent a particular respondent's replies have been.

Teachers and researchers have developed numerous behavioral checklists over the past three decades, and it can be difficult to choose an appropriate measure from all these options. One good way to narrow the choices is to review the research regarding each scale, so an informed decision can be made. A recent review (Jarosewich, Pfeiffer, & Morris, 2002) offers one helpful source for this sort of information. Multiple sources of support are better than single ones, and for obvious reasons, research conducted by individuals who are not the authors of a measure should be given more credence than research by the authors who developed a particular scale or checklist.

If parents or community members will be completing rating scales, the language in which the scales are available may also be relevant. Appendix C consists of a Spanish translation of the Scales for Identifying Gifted Students (SIGS) Home Rating Scales that can be used with speakers of Mexican Spanish. Keep in mind that Spanish, like many other languages, has a variety of dialects, and translations must be matched by dialect, as well as by language if they are to be effective. This is particularly important in the case of Spanish-language materials, because there are important vocabulary differences across dialects.

Materials translated in Spain will be different than those from Puerto Rico or Venezuela, and none of these would be fully appropriate for use with speakers of Mexican or Cuban Spanish.

Local translations of English-language assessment materials should also be avoided, as such translations can be quite difficult to perform successfully. Even when such translations are done well, the simple fact of using a different language has unpredictable effects on the validity and reliability of rating scales and other assessment measures. The interested reader is encouraged to consult Chapter 9 of the Standards for Educational and Psychological Testing (Joint Committee, 1999) for additional information on this topic.

Nonverbal Tests

Another approach to identifying gifted English Language Learners and other students from groups traditionally under-represented in programs for gifted students is the use of nonverbal tests. In essence, these are standardized tests that are characterized by minimal instructions and by test questions that utilize visual stimuli—pictures or abstract designs—rather than written language. Note that *nonverbal* refers only to the tests themselves, not to the internal thought processes the student uses to answer test items. Commonly used nonverbal tests include the Test of Nonverbal Intelligence (TONI-3; Brown, Sherbenou, & Johnsen, 1997), the Naglieri Nonverbal Intelligence Test (NNAT; Naglieri, 1996), and the oldest test of this type, the Raven's Progressive Matrices (Raven, Raven, & Court, 2000), which was first published in 1938.

Nonverbal tests appear to be a great idea, but they have limitations that may not be apparent at first glance. Although these tests tend to return smaller differences across ethnic and especially linguistic groups, they have at times been promoted as having none of the ethnicity-based score differences that are so apparent when using language-based IQ tests. (Lohman, 2005a; Naglieri & Ford, 2005). In fact, it is quite possible for a nonverbal test to be more loaded with cultural biases than a language-based test, particularly if pictures rather than abstract shapes are used. For example, a line drawing of a mailbox is easily recognized as such by most students in the United States. However, for the child living in an apartment complex or coming from another country, the same drawing may not look anything like the mailboxes that these children have experienced; in some cases, depending on their background, students from other countries may not have experienced mailboxes at all. These are the sorts of issues that keep test developers awake at night.

Another problem with nonverbal identification measures is that gifted programs rarely teach nonverbal content; in fact, most gifted programs strongly emphasize verbal skills. Some educators question the wisdom of identifying students based on a set of skills students may not actually use once they are accepted into the gifted program. This is a valid point, although it would seem appropriate for a school in this situation to offer a gifted program designed to meet the needs of such students, rather than expecting the students to fit into a preconceived program that provides a poor match to their strengths (Frasier, 1989; Rogers, 2002).

Finally, the test user should be wary if he or she happens to encounter extravagant claims made by the authors of nonverbal tests. These tests are less similar to day-to-day school activities, so they tend to be poorer predictors of academic achievement than language-based tests (Lohman, 2005b). Reliance on nonverbal tests alone could cause many students who should be in gifted programs to be missed. As Frasier (1989) and others have noted, the use of multiple measures or pathways for assessing giftedness is vital in ensuring that all students have the opportunity to demonstrate their abilities.

Dynamic Assessment

Dynamic assessment is a strategy originally developed to determine whether culturally and linguistically diverse students in Israel would be eligible for placement in special education classes (Feuerstein, Rand, & Hoffman, 1979). In essence, the method uses a pretest to determine a student's minimum level of ability, then an adult works individually with the student as he or she learns how to complete a set of similar problems. After receiving such training, a third set of problems is used as a posttest to determine the level at which the student is now capable of performing.

The advantage of this method is that it estimates students' learning potential, or ability to learn new material, rather than prior knowledge. Test items are often nonverbal in nature, minimizing the influence of English language proficiency on test results. Although developed for learning disabled students, dynamic assessment methods have also been used with gifted students and students from other diverse populations (Matthews, 2002a; Swanson & Lussier, 2001). Except for the level of difficulty of the materials, there is little difference in how dynamic assessment methods are conducted within gifted versus learning disabled populations. Some gifted students are likely to score quite well on the pretest, which means that pretest, as well as posttest, scores must be considered when seeking to identify gifted students using this approach. The Swanson-Cognitive Processing Test (S-CPT; Swanson, 1996) is the only commercially available measure of intelligence that utilizes this approach to assessment.

Disadvantages of the dynamic assessment method include its experimental nature; the time needed to work individually with each student; and the lack of standardization of training protocols, scoring procedures, and other aspects that are commonly standardized on traditionally formatted tests. Several experimental tests (e.g., Tzuriel, 2001) and at least one commercially published measure (Swanson, 1996) have been developed based on these methods, and future development studies may address these drawbacks and produce a more useful application of this approach. Consult Lidz and Elliott (2000), Sternberg & Grigorenko (2002), and Tzuriel for further information regarding this method.

Promoting Testing Success for ELL Students

It should be amply clear by this point that testing alone is insufficient for identifying gifted English Language Learners.

However, the classroom teacher usually has limited influence in determining how gifted students are identified. These decisions are generally made at the state and district level. Standardized aptitude (IQ) or achievement tests remain the primary means of qualifying students for gifted programs. However, there are still steps teachers can take to help ELL students prepare for standardized testing. Remember, these strategies are not intended to "teach to" the test; rather, the intention is to help students effectively convey what they already know. Highly able students will be capable of learning these strategies quickly. The first of these strategies concerns the language of testing. Standardized tests contain predictable patterns of language use, and these are often distinct from standard spoken English. A set of questioning patterns will tend to appear repeatedly within a particular test, with some variation in order. For example, there are many words that may be used to present a subtraction problem. Words including *minus, take away from*, and *less* may all be directing students toward the same arithmetic operation. All students may have trouble understanding that these varied wordings have the same meaning, but ELL students are particularly prone to such difficulties. Practice tests and released versions of tests offer a good source for finding examples of the particular sorts of wordings students may face.

The second strategic area concerns the contextual clues in the test itself. These include such things as words that are italicized or underlined, providing clues about the type of answer that will be considered correct. Words such as *best* or *not* are used to convey particular meanings; best implies that more than one multiple-choice answer may be correct, while not may mean that all but one of the answers are correct (Rivera & Stansfield, 2004). These sorts of skills, traditionally described as "test smarts," can and should be taught to all students.

The third strategic area involves familiarity with the test itself. Because few other countries are as concerned with testing as the United States, students from other countries may have little familiarity with tests or the testing process. Especially for younger children, testing can be quite intimidating. Even activities that many people take for granted, such as filling in bubbles with a No. 2 pencil, can stifle some students. Teachers need to work with ELL students to develop familiarity with the test forms and the testing process, so that these students will be able to put forth their best efforts when encountering a testing situation.

Program Models Serving English Language Learners

Schools have developed a wide variety of approaches for educating English Language Learners. Based on the cognitive and social benefits of additive bilingualism, program models that encourage children's development in more than one language are more valuable than programs that seek to develop one language at the expense of the other (Baker, 2000). Thus, following Baker, the program models presented here are described as either "stronger" or "weaker." Schools use each of these approaches, and sometimes a hybrid of one or more of them. The particular program model a school uses can have some influence on the ability to find gifted ELL students.

How can educators determine which of the various models might be appropriate for their school? This can be a difficult question, but some guidelines have been developed for this purpose. The materials by Burkart and Sheppard (see resources), available online, may be quite helpful for those who are searching for guidance in this area. To summarize the advice they offer, Federal, state, and local laws may constrain your school's available options. Once you have determined the legal requirements you will have to meet, the next step is to determine the degree and type of language support your program will be able to offer to students. This question should be considered with regard to instruction in the students' native language, as well as to English learning. Finally, the needs of students in your particular setting provide the other important piece of information. Once you have addressed these questions, you will be able to consider whether each of the program options in the sections that follow might be an appropriate fit for your school.

Foreign Language Immersion Programs

Stronger approaches are those that promote two or more languages equally. These also tend to promote bilingual literacy and bi- or multicultural values. Foreign language immersion programs are usually designed to teach English-monolingual students a second language by offering instruction partially or completely in the second language. Because these programs primarily serve mainstream students, gifted identification processes and programs do not need to differ from those in ordinary schools, apart from perhaps having a stronger focus on verbal abilities.

Dual Language Programs

Dual language programs are similar to foreign language immersion programs, except these offer two languages and split instructional time between the two. For example, each classroom may be taught in Spanish in the mornings and in English in the afternoons. Dual language schools often seek to have a student body evenly split between native speakers of each language, and because these schools may serve an entire district, admission is often competitive. In theory, both languages and cultures will be valued equally in such an arrangement, although in practice this can be difficult to achieve. Students who come to such programs speaking the nonmainstream language at home tend to do well, and these environments may provide a fertile source of gifted students from both mainstream and nonmainstream backgrounds.

Sheltered Content Instruction

Sheltered content instruction is another type of transitional program providing a few hours of instruction each day or week, offering ESOL instruction integrated with content area instruction. As is the case with pullout gifted programs, the time students spend in sheltered content instruction can vary widely from one school to the next. Well-designed sheltered instruction programs can be quite effective in promoting academic achievement, because students are less likely to fall behind in the content areas than they are in other types of transitional programs (Echevarria, Vogt, & Short, 2004).

Heritage Language Programs

Heritage language programs may offer instruction to language minority students in their home language, sometimes supplemented with instruction in English, tailored to students' educational needs in each language (Matthews & Matthews, 2004). These programs are relatively uncommon in the United States, but are potentially outstanding sources for identifying high ability within the student populations they serve (Matthews & Matthews).

English Immersion Programs

Weaker approaches favor English acquisition at the expense of developing abilities in both languages. The aim of these programs is usually the assimilation of students into the dominant monolingual culture. English immersion programs, also called submersion programs by their many critics, essentially drop students into English-only settings where students either sink or swim. The term *immersion* can be confusing, because it may also be applied without modifiers to programs that teach students other languages. Immersion programs have been successful in some contexts, such as teaching French to English–speaking Canadian students. In the U.S., however, where other languages do not share the high status that French has in Canada, immersion programs that focus on English generally come at the expense of the second or home language.

Transitional Bilingual Programs

Transitional bilingual programs offer students a year or two of instruction in their home language, often for only part of the day, and are designed to transition students rapidly to all-English instruction. These programs may include pullout ESOL instruction, offering students individualized instruction in the English language for a few hours each day or week, as well as newcomer programs that focus on acclimating students to the school context in the U.S.

Care must be taken that peers do not stigmatize students for attending special classes; this caution also applies to special classes for gifted students. Other concerns these programs share in common with gifted education include issues of teacher training, access to peers, and de facto segregation.

Unfortunately, it generally takes 3–7 years for children to learn English well enough to use it effectively in the classroom setting, so these weaker approaches often place English Language Learners at a competitive disadvantage. Gifted or highly motivated students in these programs may make the transition to English proficiency more quickly than their peers, but in the absence of additional content learning in their first language or effective sheltered instruction programs, they unlikely will be capable of achieving the high test scores often required for admission into gifted programs.

Supporting Language Acquisition in the Classroom

Although available program options vary widely in effectiveness, there are a number of things teachers can do to support their students' language acquisition. By using these strategies to enrich instruction, it will be more likely that ELL students will be able to qualify for gifted program entry. These may be used in the regular classroom, as well as for developing skills of students in a pregifted program setting (Aguirre, 2003). These strategies may also be used with ELL students who already participate in a gifted class, particularly if the student qualified on the basis of math scores, but still has relatively low verbal scores.

Several categories of environmental factors appear to have an influence on second language acquisition. These include the naturalness of the environment, the learner's role in communication, the availability of concrete referents, and the English language models available (Piper, 2003). Successful language learning environments create a natural context for language use, rather than emphasizing formal rules and drills, and they allow for learners to participate in two-way communication. Concrete referents are simply objects that can be observed while learning new words; these increase understanding by providing an immediate meaning to go with the new vocabulary. The English language models are the individuals the ELL child looks to for examples of the new language. Children seem to prefer to use peers rather than adults for this purpose (Piper). Even classrooms with only a few ELL students can be arranged to take advantage of these environmental principles, thereby allowing students to fully develop and express their abilities.

There are other important instructional strategies that can be used by all classroom teachers working with English Language Learners. These include:

- creating a natural context for practicing language skills,
- selecting activities that involve two-way communication,
- using concrete objects to help learn vocabulary,
- providing students the opportunity to interact with native speakers who are good language models,
- utilizing gestures and facial expressions to add meaning,
- employing repetition and summarization to increase understanding, and
- minimizing the time the teacher spends talking to the class.

Teachers can provide a scaffold for the English language acquisition process by providing contextual support for instructions, using facial expressions and other gestures to add meaning to their words. Consciously repeating, summarizing, and restating directions can also increase ELL students' comprehension of new material and their awareness of different ways that a thought may be expressed in English. Finally, note that a combination of indirect and direct instruction techniques appears to be more effective than either strategy alone for improving students' academic English abilities.

Piper (2003) offers examples of other instructional strategies that should be avoided. Chief among these are teacher-centered or teacher-directed conversations, which in some classrooms may take up more than half of the available instructional time. When teachers are talking, students are not; yet, students learn language best by using it. Piper also stresses that schools should teach students what they do not yet know, yet many classrooms emphasize repetition of tasks that students already have mastered. Although this practice holds back all students, it is particularly harmful to gifted children who may develop achievement problems as a result. For concrete examples of appropriate and inappropriate classroom practices, consult Chapter 10 in Piper's book.

Building Services for Gifted ELLs

A school's existing gifted education program will provide a framework within which to build services for gifted English Language Learners. Following are two possible situations with a description of circumstances that might be encountered in each. Most schools will likely fall somewhere between these two extremes, thus efforts can be adjusted accordingly.

Generally speaking gifted programs are designed to serve the top 5–10% of students, but their target population may vary from less than 1% to 30% or more depending on the program model. The particular student population present in a school may also have a strong influence on how many students participate in such a program. Programs that seek to enroll the top 10% of students (based on statewide criteria) may serve no students at all, or may serve 25% or more of students depending on the particular school in question. The affluence of the school population, its ethnic makeup, and the nature of the surrounding community all influence whether and how gifted programs are established, as well as the resources these are allotted in comparison to other school programs.

Some schools serving high-poverty or high-immigration areas may have no gifted program at all. These may be in a state that does not fund gifted education, or has no mandate for such programs. It may also be that no students have qualified under the established guidelines, so a school receives no gifted program funding. Parent and community support for gifted education tends to be low at schools in these situations. Whatever the cause, the attitudes of other school personnel, particularly among the administration, should be determined. In these environments, the mistaken assumption that "we have no gifted students at our school" is all too commonly expressed. However, a handful of concerned teachers or administrators who take action can change this perception. The advantage to not having a gifted program is that one may be established and can be designed from the ground up to meet the needs of students in a particular school.

All schools have some children who are more capable learners, and others who are not as capable. If a school's most capable students do not qualify for gifted services, one effective strategy involves providing pullout enrichment classes for these students so they will be able to qualify in a future year. This strategy is particularly effective with younger elementary students, who have several years at the same school ahead of them. Teacher ratings, particularly using scales such as the one in Appendix B, can be used in combination with standardized test scores to identify the students who could benefit from such classes.

Alternatively, you may find a school has a strong gifted program that primarily serves mainstream students. Schools that are 80% minority may have gifted programs in which 95% of the enrollment is mainstream students. Not only does this cast gifted programs in an unflattering light, making them appear elitist or even racist, but it also suggests that quite a few highly able students are being overlooked in the selection process. Change is clearly needed in such situations, but strong gifted programs serving mainstream students tend to have powerful and well-connected community and parent networks. As many southeastern states' experiences demonstrate, these networks may object strongly to efforts they perceive as "lowering standards" (Golden, 2004; Matthews, 2001). Effective public relations strategies, both within the school and in the community, are a key element in promoting positive change and in advocating successfully for gifted education (Besnoy, 2005).

States, districts, and schools are now beginning to implement a wide variety of approaches to help diversify existing programs for the gifted, and in time the more effective among these models will make their way into the best practices literature. For the present, there are many different approaches that may be successful in diversifying existing programs for the gifted. The best approach will be one that is research-based and also takes into account the characteristics and needs of a particular student body and school.

Differentiating Classroom Instruction for Gifted ELLs

Multilevel classes, which require teaching to students at different levels within a single classroom, are a common approach to serving gifted children. Although this heterogeneous grouping approach appears to be less effective for gifted students in comparison with other types of ability grouping (Kulik & Kulik, 1992), schools favor grouping students in this manner because it requires few additional resources. Such grouping requires teachers to differentiate instruction for students who are capable of working at levels that are higher (or lower) than average (Smutny, Walker, & Meckstroth, 1997).

This differentiation can be a difficult task, and observations suggest that gifted students' needs may not be met in such a setting if high-stakes testing causes the teacher's attention to be focused mostly on the needs of lower-performing students.

Consider, however, that teaching to the top learners of the class rather than to the middle or bottom may raise the performance of students in the middle while keeping the top students from being bored. Peer effects on achievement are quite strong, especially at the elementary level (Betts et al., 2003), and high-achieving students are likely to bring up their peers by association. In addition, schools tend to have more resources available to help students at the bottom of their class than those for the underachieving student whose performance may remain at or above average.

For the ELL child who is not formally identified as gifted, a heterogeneous classroom may allow the child to work with other able students who would be less accessible if there were a pullout gifted program. In such cases, the same sorts of teaching strategies may be used as with mainstream gifted students, with the addition of teacher sensitivity to cultural differences in how students interact and express themselves. For mainstream gifted students in the regular classroom, Smutny et al. (1997) recommend helping children to work comfortably with one another, providing a balance of structure and creativity, incorporating sensitivity to individual learning styles, assessing the child's knowledge base when planning instruction, and providing a balance between group and independent activities. Effective instruction shares many of these same general features, no matter which children are being taught. Gifted students simply need more of some features (such as curricular depth, breadth, or complexity), yet less of others (repetition, for example).

Final Thoughts

It takes a special blend of knowledge, commitment, and activism to effectively support gifted English Language Learners in today's public schools. By the time you have read this far you have become part of a select, yet growing, group of educators who are dedicated to making a difference in the lives of these students. Remember that each child you help to reach his or her potential may go on to help others in turn, and the full results of your efforts may not be visible for many years to come. Even the largest trees were once tiny seeds and would not be where they are today had they not taken root in an appropriate nurturing environment. Your efforts will make a difference.

Annotated Web Resources

Basic Interpersonal Communicative Skills (BICS) and Cognitive Academic Language Proficiency (CALP)
http://www.iteachilearn.com/cummins/bicscalp.html

Jim Cummins is one of the best-known researchers studying language acquisition and education. On this Web site he discusses BICS and CALP, the explanatory model he developed to explain why children often appear to be verbally fluent in a new language long before they are able to function academically in the new language. Many of Cummins' writings are also available online through this Web site: http://ourworld.compuserve.com/homepages/ JWCRAWFORD

Davidson Institute for Talent Development
http://www.ditd.org/public

The Davidson Institute administers scholarship programs for profoundly gifted youth, publishes an electronic newsletter about gifted education, and publicizes the founders' book, *Genius Denied: How to Stop Wasting Our Brightest Young Minds.* Follow the link to the Genius Denied Web site to find a map listing gifted education policies by state.

Do You Speak American?
http://www.pbs.org/speak

This is the Web site for the companion PBS series about language in the United States. Of particular interest to teachers, the site features five curriculum units for high school age students, including a unit on Spanish and Chicano English. The descriptions of other American dialects are especially useful, as are the pages about language prestige and language prejudice.

Leung, A. K. C., & Kao, C. P. (1999). Evaluation and management of the child with speech delay. *American Family Physician 59*, 3121–3139.
http://www.aafp.org/afp/990600ap/3121.html

This article, written for doctors, gives a comprehensive introduction to speech delay. These authors note that bilingualism can sometimes cause delayed speech in one or both languages even when comprehension is normal for the age in both languages. Parents should be aware that children with speech delays due to bilingualism usually become proficient in both languages before age 5.

The Center for Applied Linguistics
http://www.cal.org

The Center for Applied Linguistics (CAL) is a nonprofit organization of scholars and educators who study linguistics for the purpose of identifying and addressing language-related problems. CAL was one of the first organizations working to develop research-based materials for English as a second language and foreign language instruction.

The National Association for Bilingual Education
http://www.nabe.org

> The National Association for Bilingual Education (NABE) is a national professional organization representing both English Language Learners and professionals working in bilingual education. The Association's Web site has information about research and advocacy efforts, and NABE sponsors an annual conference that is well attended by researchers and teachers in the area of bilingual education.

National Center for English Language Acquisition's
State Pages
http://www.ncela.gwu.edu/policy/states/index.htm

> This site, a part of the National Center for English Language Acquisition and Language Instruction Educational Programs, gives state-by-state listings of educational policies and practices related to English Language Learners. The site includes links to state departments of education and information about demographic trends within each state.

Language Links: A New World of Understanding
http://polyglot.lss.wisc.edu/lss/lang/langlink.html

> This site features annotated links to Web sites for language teachers and language learners. Of particular interest are links to Web-based teaching activities arranged by language (includes ESL/EFL), although these are mostly appropriate for older students.

Universal Declaration of Linguistic Rights
http://www.unesco.org/most/lnngo11.htm

> Representatives of almost 90 nations signed this declaration, which affirms that all people should have the right to use their native language. For example, Article 26 states the following:

> All language communities are entitled to an education
> which will enable their members to acquire a full com-
> mand of their own language, including the different
> abilities relating to all the usual spheres of use, as well as
> the most extensive possible command of any other lan-
> guage they may wish to know. (UNESCO, 1996, ¶ 75)

For a more impassioned view of this topic, the reader may
also wish to consult Skuttnab-Kangas' criticism (2000) of
this UNESCO declaration.

Annotated Print Resources

Baker, C. (2000). *A parents' and teachers' guide to bilingualism* (2nd
ed.). Clevedon, England: Multilingual Matters.

Baker, C. (2001). *Foundations of bilingual education and bilingualism* (3rd ed.). Clevedon, England: Multilingual Matters.

In these two textbooks, Colin Baker offers an introduction
to bilingualism and bilingual education. The parents' and
teachers' guide uses a question and answer format to
address the most commonly raised questions about raising
children bilingually. The *Foundations* book is larger and
more comprehensive, and guides the reader who may
know little about these topics toward an in-depth understanding of these important social and educational issues.
Both texts cite relevant research in support of the author's
claims, and both are applicable to all language combina-
tions.

Baldwin, A. Y., & Vialle, W. (Eds.). (1999). *The many faces of
giftedness: Lifting the masks.* Belmont, CA: Wadsworth
Publishing Company.

The first four chapters of this book, two of which focus on
the United States and two on Australia, will prove the most
useful for many readers. These chapters consider cultural

issues, identification practices, and teaching strategies for specific groups of students.

Bernal, E. M., & Reyna, J. (1974). *Analysis of giftedness in Mexican American children and design of a prototype identification instrument.* Austin, TX: Southwest Educational Development Laboratory.

This report was the first research investigating giftedness among Mexican American students. Students from three cities in Texas, including 108 Spanish/English bilingual students, participated in these studies. The sample behavior rating scale presented in Appendix A was developed in the course of this project.

Burkart, G. S., & Sheppard, K. (n.d.). *Content-ESL across the USA: A training packet.* Retrieved August 1, 2005, from http://www.ncela.gwu.edu/pubs/cal/contentesl

The 15 content-ESL guides in this series are a wonderful resource for anyone who is creating or modifying an ESL program. Topics range from evaluation of assessment practices to sample lesson plans and guidelines for adapting instructional materials. The second guide, which covers designing, implementing, and sustaining content-ESL programs, is particularly useful.

Castellano, J. A., & Díaz, E. I. (Eds.). (2002). *Reaching new horizons: Gifted and talented education for culturally and linguistically diverse students.* Boston: Allyn & Bacon.

Castellano, J. A. (Ed.). (2003). *Special populations in gifted education: Working with diverse gifted learners.* Boston: Allyn & Bacon.

Chapters in these edited volumes discuss most of the issues related to diversity in gifted education. Particular chapters cover identification, assessment, and program models for finding and serving gifted students who are linguistically diverse. Reviews of successful programs and the descriptions of classroom approaches for serving bilingual gifted and talented students are a particularly helpful component in the 2002 volume.

Diaz Soto, L. (Ed.). (2002). *Making a difference in the lives of bilingual/bicultural children.* New York: Peter Lang.

The authors in this edited book offer critical postmodern perspectives on the education of bilingual and bicultural children. A particular strength of this text is its inclusion of a wide variety of linguistic and cultural backgrounds, including Native American and immigrant Chinese children.

Ellis, R. (1997). *Second language acquisition.* Oxford: Oxford University Press.

Ellis offers a concise introduction to second language acquisition in this small volume. A glossary of terms and an annotated bibliography are quite helpful for anyone just learning about this topic.

Echevarria, J., Vogt, M. E., & Short, D. J. (2004). *Making content comprehensible to English learners: The SIOP model* (2nd ed.). Boston: Allyn & Bacon.

SIOP is the Sheltered Instruction Observation Protocol, a research-based model for using sheltered delivery of content instruction to ELL students in the mainstream classroom. The text uses vignettes to illustrate each component of the SIOP model in effective and less effective implementations, and offers concrete guidance on instructional delivery and program assessment.

Esquivel, G. B., & Houtz, J. C. (Eds.). (2000). *Creativity and giftedness in culturally diverse students.* Cresskill, NJ: Hampton Press.

Creativity is frequently listed as an area of strength common to diverse gifted students. Selections in this book review the literature that supports this assertion, and describe the socio-emotional, linguistic, and cognitive characteristics that educators may expect to encounter among their culturally and linguistically diverse students.

Ford, D. Y., & Harris III, J. J. (1999). *Multicultural gifted education*. New York: Teachers College Press.

These authors synthesize the fields of multicultural and gifted education. They offer suggestions for evaluating the multicultural content of existing programs, and present sample activities and best practices for multicultural gifted students and programs.

Goldstein, T. (2003). *Teaching and learning in a multilingual school: Choices, risks, and dilemmas*. Mahwah, NJ: Lawrence Erlbaum Associates.

This book presents a case study of a Canadian high school and how it responded to a rapid influx of Cantonese-speaking immigrant students. Chapters are oriented topically, and each ends with a short section designed to elicit reflection and discussion. This book probably would be quite useful for professional development purposes at any school that is experiencing rapid changes to its student demographics.

Gonzalez, V. (Ed.). (1999). *Language and cognitive development in second language learning: Educational implications for children and adults*. Boston: Allyn & Bacon.

Gonzalez focuses on academic research in this publication, placing a strong emphasis on the assessment of bilingual students. Although they are not light reading, the articles give a good picture of how research may be used to improve school practices.

González, M. L., Huerta-Macías, A., & Tinajero, J. V. (Eds.). (1998). *Educating Latino students: A guide to successful practice.* Lancaster, PA: Technomic Publishing.

Many of the sections in this book seem to be aimed primarily at principals, but are probably also relevant to the classroom teacher. Descriptions of effective learning environments and effective approaches to assessment and standardized testing may be particularly useful to teachers. The chapter "Issues in the Teaching of Math and Science to Latinos" is one of few available resources on this topic.

Hall, J. K., & Eggington, W. G. (Eds.). (2000). *The sociopolitics of English language teaching.* Clevedon, England: Multicultural Matters.

This collection of papers addresses the social, cultural, and political issues surrounding English language teaching and learning. Chapters on the "Official English" movement, nonnative varieties of English, and the politics of language in the classroom may be particularly of interest.

Howard, G. R. (1999). *We can't teach what we don't know: White teachers, multiracial schools.* New York: Teachers College Press.

The author describes his personal path toward developing multicultural awareness, and goes on to discuss White identity and its relationship to educational practice. This is a relatively short book that does a good job of holding the readers' attention as it raises important issues.

Johnson, K. R. (1999). *How did you get to be Mexican? A White/Brown man's search for identity.* Philadelphia: Temple University Press.

Johnson has a mixed Latino and Anglo heritage and he describes how this racial identity influenced his personal development. By discussing his educational journey, leading to becoming a law professor, Johnson effectively raises issues of cultural assimilation, race relations, and diversity in the context of American society.

Kogan, E. (2001). *Gifted bilingual students: A paradox?* New York: Peter Lang.

Kogan considers important issues in gifted bilingual education in the United States, including identification practices and parent involvement. She also presents three case studies of gifted bilingual students, highlighting the varied experiences that these students may face in school.

Lessow-Hurley, J. (2003). *Meeting the needs of second language learners: An educator's guide.* Alexandria, VA: Association for Supervision and Curriculum Development.

This concise book introduces multilingual education and debunks some of the most common misconceptions about these issues. It also describes the most commonly used models in language education, summarizes relevant legal decisions, and goes over the training that teachers should have to work with second language learners.

López Carrasco, M. Á. (1994). *Estudio, mito y realidad del niño sobredotado.* [Study, myth and reality of the gifted child]. Puebla, Pue., México: Universidad Iberoamericana Golfo Central/Lupus Inquisidor.

López Carrasco reflects on his own upbringing as a gifted child in Mexico and presents an introduction to the characteristics and needs of gifted students. This book is available in Spanish only, but may represent a useful resource for Spanish-speaking audiences.

Piper, T. (2003). *Language and learning: The home and school years* (3rd ed.). Upper Saddle River, NJ: Merrill.
Piper's textbook provides a comprehensive yet straightfor-

ward introduction to first and second language acquisition, with a focus on how the process takes place for young children. In the final chapter, 10 principles are offered to help teachers develop their own effective classroom instruction.

Reis, S. M., & Renzulli, J. S. (2005). *Curriculum compacting: An easy start to differentiating for high-potential students.* Waco, TX: Prufrock Press.

In this book, another volume of the Practical Strategies Series, Reis and Renzulli offer a brief, yet well-rounded introduction to curriculum compacting. This approach can and should be used with gifted English Language Learners enrolled in the regular classroom.

Slocumb, P. D., & Payne, R. K. (2000). *Removing the mask: Giftedness in poverty.* Highlands, TX: RFT Publishing Co.

This book, used by the authors to conduct professional development workshops, introduces teachers to some of the differences they may encounter when working with gifted students from impoverished backgrounds. Because many ELL students also come from home environments in poverty, this book may also be helpful to teachers working with these children.

Strip, C. A. (with Hirsch, G.). (2000). *Ayudando a niños dotados a volar: Una guía práctica para padres y maestros.* [Helping gifted children soar: A practical guide for parents and teachers]. Scottsdale, AZ: Gifted Psychology Press.

This introduction to gifted education is available in both English and Spanish versions. It may be particularly useful for offering Spanish-language guidance when making educational decisions about gifted children.

Tokuhama-Espinosa, T. (2001). *Raising multilingual children: Foreign language acquisition and children.* Westport, CT: Bergin & Garvey.

This unique book develops an analogy comparing baking to raising multilingual children. Although based on research, the book is primarily a how-to guide for families. Examples are drawn from a wide variety of bi- and multilingual situations. Many of the recommended strategies could readily be adapted for classroom use.

Torrance, E. P., Goff, K., & Satterfield, N. B. (1998). *Multicultural mentoring of the gifted and talented.* Waco, TX: Prufrock Press.

This book introduces the reader to all aspects of mentoring, with a focus on fostering success in multicultural settings. Chapter 2 in particular addresses racial, cultural, and economic differences and how awareness of these issues can lead to a more successful mentoring relationship.

Valdés, G. (1996). *Con respeto: Bridging the distance between culturally diverse families and schools: An ethnographic portrait.* New York: Teachers College Press.

Valdés uses case studies to convey the experiences of 10 immigrant Mexican families whose children are attending school in the border regions of the United States. These families' experiences and feelings show how failure to take cultural differences into account can hamper schools' efforts to serve these children.

Valdés, G. (Ed.). (2003). *Expanding definitions of giftedness: The case of young interpreters from immigrant communities.* Mahwah, NJ: Lawrence Erlbaum Associates.

This book proposes an innovative new direction in gifted education, suggesting that "youngsters who are selected to serve as family interpreters perform at remarkably high levels of accomplishment when compared with others of their age, experience, and environment, and should thus clearly be seen as included" in definitions of giftedness (pg. xix). Everyone interested in gifted ELL students should read this.

Wortham, S., Murillo E. G., Jr., & Hamann, E. T. (Eds.). (2001). *Education in the new Latino diaspora: Policy and the politics of identity.* Westport, CT: Ablex Publishing.

Multiple case studies document the experiences of Latino immigrants who move to parts of the United States that have not historically had a Latino presence, hence the "New Latino Diaspora." The authors consider not only the points of view of the immigrants themselves, but also the responses of the local communities to their arrival.

Zentella, A. C. (1997). *Growing up bilingual: Puerto Rican children in New York.* Malden, MA: Blackwell Publishers.

The case studies in this book illuminate the processes of constructing bilingual identities and socializing children into language communities, within the context of the Puerto Rican community in New York. The book also discusses the linguistic amalgam commonly referred to as "Spanglish."

Appendix A: Sample Language Background Survey

Directions: For each individual listed in Column 1, ask the student what language(s) the person speaks to the student, and what language(s) the student uses to speak to the person. For an English/Spanish bilingual student, responses might be either English, Spanish, or both languages.

Language Background Survey Student Code_____

Person	Language you speak to them	Language they speak to you
Mother		
Father		
Brother(s)		
Sister(s)		
Aunt/Uncle		
Grandparents		
Babysitter		
Friends		

*Birthplace_____   *Years in U.S._____

*These two items provide useful perspective, but are not strictly necessary and may be sensitive to some individuals. Use with discretion.

Note. From *Dynamic Assessment of Academic Ability of Bilingual Immigrant Latino Children* by M. S. Matthews, 2002, Doctoral dissertation, University of Georgia. Copyright ©2002 by M. S. Matthews. Reprinted with permission.

Appendix B: SIGS Home Rating Scales

Scale 1: General Intellectual Ability

	Never	Rarely	Some	Somewhat More	Much More
1. Has excellent reasoning ability.	0	1	2	3	4
2. Establishes cause-effect relationships easily.	0	1	2	3	4
3. Can analyze an issue from many points of view.	0	1	2	3	4
4. Is able to reach good conclusions based on evidence.	0	1	2	3	4
5. Is curious and seeks answers to questions.	0	1	2	3	4
6. Is an excellent planner and decision maker.	0	1	2	3	4
7. Gathers information to make sense of a situation.	0	1	2	3	4
8. Demonstrates a healthy skepticism and curiosity.	0	1	2	3	4
9. Asks complex questions about a topic.	0	1	2	3	4
10. Is able to rapidly understand novel tasks.	0	1	2	3	4
11. Is able to figure out what is needed to solve a problem.	0	1	2	3	4
12. Can easily relate new information to old information.	0	1	2	3	4

TOTAL: ☐ = 0 + ___ + ___ + ___ + ___

Scale 2: Language Arts

Note. For items relating to expressive language, the statement refers to both spoken and written language. For example: "Has an advanced vocabulary" can refer to an advanced spoken vocabulary or an advanced written vocabulary.

1. Has an advanced vocabulary.	0	1	2	3	4
2. Reads competently and often.	0	1	2	3	4
3. Uses sophisticated syntax (i.e., the way in which words are put together).	0	1	2	3	4
4. Enjoys talking about ideas or feelings generated by what is read or what is read to him or her.	0	1	2	3	4
5. Prefers advanced-level books; enjoys difficult reading material.	0	1	2	3	4
6. Explains precisely and clearly.	0	1	2	3	4
7. Reads or speaks with expression to create meaning.	0	1	2	3	4
8. Uses language in unusual or novel ways.	0	1	2	3	4
9. Reads critically (i.e., reads with careful judgement and evaluation).	0	1	2	3	4
10. Uses mature themes and vocabulary.	0	1	2	3	4
11. Can find many ways to express ideas so that others will understand.	0	1	2	3	4
12. Is able to discuss literature or other issues at an interpretative (explanatory) level.	0	1	2	3	4

TOTAL: ☐ = 0 + ___ + ___ + ___ + ___

Scale 3: Mathematics

1. Recognizes mathematical patterns and relationships (e.g. extends a sequence of numbers; analyzes how two numbers "go together").	0	1	2	3	4
2. Applies ideas form one mathematical problem to another.	0	1	2	3	4
3. Is persistent in finding solutions to mathematical problems.	0	1	2	3	4
4. Understands mathematical principles quickly.	0	1	2	3	4
5. Easily distinguishes between relevant and irrelevant information in mathematical problems.	0	1	2	3	4
6. Uses creative or unusual strategies to solve mathematical problems.	0	1	2	3	4
7. Is successful with advanced-level mathematical concepts.	0	1	2	3	4
8. Develops multiple strategies to solve mathematical problems.	0	1	2	3	4
9. Uses correct mathematical language.	0	1	2	3	4
10. Has knowledge about a variety of mathematical topics.	0	1	2	3	4
11. Is discovery oriented (i.e., likes to find answers to mathematical problems).	0	1	2	3	4
12. Intuitively knows the answer to many mathematical problems.	0	1	2	3	4

TOTAL: ☐ = 0 + ___ + ___ + ___ + ___

Appendix B: SIGS Home Rating Scales, continued

Scale 4: Science

	Never	Rarely	Some	Somewhat More	Much More
1. Enjoys investigating and exploring science-related topics.	0	1	2	3	4
2. Is able to formulate sound hypotheses based on evidence.	0	1	2	3	4
3. Understands the scientific process.	0	1	2	3	4
4. Asks analytical questions (i.e., questions about the elements or parts of a problem).	0	1	2	3	4
5. Initiates science investigations on own.	0	1	2	3	4
6. Is observant; sees details.	0	1	2	3	4
7. Can apply a scientific finding from one situation to another.	0	1	2	3	4
8. Effective in deductive reasoning (i.e., can start with the big idea and break it into parts).	0	1	2	3	4
9. Can quickly figure out cause-and-effect relationships.	0	1	2	3	4
10. Observes events closely.	0	1	2	3	4
11. Understands how scientific events are related.	0	1	2	3	4
12. Is persistent in conducting scientific investigations.	0	1	2	3	4

TOTAL: ☐ = 0 + __ + __ + __ + __

Scale 5: Social Studies

	Never	Rarely	Some	Somewhat More	Much More
1. Has an intense curiosity about world and current events.	0	1	2	3	4
2. Makes judgments based on right and wrong.	0	1	2	3	4
3. Enjoys nonfiction books about social studies topics.	0	1	2	3	4
4. Makes connections between the past and present.	0	1	2	3	4
5. Appreciates the differences among world cultures.	0	1	2	3	4
6. Recognizes how cultures are related (e.g., individual to family, government to society).	0	1	2	3	4
7. Seeks to understand why people, cultures, or groups act the way they do.	0	1	2	3	4
8. Has a passion for a particular period of history (e.g., Crusades, Civil War).	0	1	2	3	4
9. Understands the importance of using trustworthy sources.	0	1	2	3	4
10. Desires to develop solutions to social problems.	0	1	2	3	4
11. Seeks to understand issues from many points of view.	0	1	2	3	4
12. Has an understanding of how people's environments affect their lifestyles.	0	1	2	3	4

TOTAL: ☐ = 0 + __ + __ + __ + __

Scale 6: Creativity

	Never	Rarely	Some	Somewhat More	Much More
1. Seeks to create rather than imitate.	0	1	2	3	4
2. Is persistent in finding solutions to problems.	0	1	2	3	4
3. Is proficient at problem finding.	0	1	2	3	4
4. Enjoys taking risks (e.g., doesn't mind consequences of being different, not afraid to try something new).	0	1	2	3	4
5. Breaks gender stereotypes.	0	1	2	3	4
6. Does not mind uncertainty.	0	1	2	3	4
7. Enjoys time along (particularly when engaged in the creative process).	0	1	2	3	4
8. Is an excellent improviser.	0	1	2	3	4
9. Has a passionate interest or talent (e.g., art, poetry, creative writing, or science).	0	1	2	3	4
10. Is attracted to the complex and unique.	0	1	2	3	4
11. Likes adventure; is energetic.	0	1	2	3	4
12. Values own creativity.	0	1	2	3	4

TOTAL: ☐ = 0 + __ + __ + __ + __

Appendix B: SIGS Home Rating Scales, continued

Scale 7: Leadership

	Never	Rarely	Some	Somewhat More	Much More
1. Is sought out by peers for advice, companionship, and ideas.	0	1	2	3	4
2. Is sensitive to the needs and concerns of others.	0	1	2	3	4
3. Adjusts easily to new situations.	0	1	2	3	4
4. Is considered a "peacemaker" by peers.	0	1	2	3	4
5. Has self-discipline.	0	1	2	3	4
6. Has an advanced level of ethical and moral understanding (i.e., knows right from wrong).	0	1	2	3	4
7. Is goal oriented.	0	1	2	3	4
8. Inspires loyalty from others.	0	1	2	3	4
9. Is supportive of peers.	0	1	2	3	4
10. Is viewed as fair or caring.	0	1	2	3	4
11. Has high ideals.	0	1	2	3	4
12. Expresses concern for and interest in community and world issues.	0	1	2	3	4

TOTAL: [   ] = 0 + ___ + ___ + ___ + ___

Summary of Scores:

	Raw Score	Standard Score	Percentile Rank
General Intellectual Ability			
Language Arts			
Mathematics			
Science			
Social Studies			
Creativity			
Leadership			

Appendix C: SIGS Home Rating Scales—Spanish

Escala 1: habilidad Intelectual General

	Nunca	Rara Vez	Igual	Algo Más	Mucho Más
1. Tiene excelente habilidad de razonamiento.	0	1	2	3	4
2. Establece fácilmente relaciones de causa y efecto.	0	1	2	3	4
3. Puede analizar una cuestión desde muchos puntos de vista.	0	1	2	3	4
4. Logra llegar a buenas conclusiones basándolas en evidencia.	0	1	2	3	4
5. Es curioso/a y busca respuestas a preguntas.	0	1	2	3	4
6. Tiene facilidad para planear y tomar decisiones.	0	1	2	3	4
7. Acumula información para entender bien una situación.	0	1	2	3	4
8. Demuestra escepticismo y curiosidad sana.	0	1	2	3	4
9. Hace preguntas complejas acerca de un tema.	0	1	2	3	4
10. Puede comprender rápidamente nuevas tareas.	0	1	2	3	4
11. Puede descifrar lo necesario para resolver un problema.	0	1	2	3	4
12. Fácilmente puede relacionar nueva información con información conocida.	0	1	2	3	4

TOTAL: ☐ = 0 + ___ + ___ + ___ + ___

Escala 2: Lenguaje

Nota. Para articulos relacionados al lenguaje expresivo, la declaración se refiere tanto al lenguaje hablado como escrito. Por ejemplo, "Tiene vocabulario avanzado" puede referirse al vocabulario hablado avanzado o al vocabulario escrito avanzado.

1. Tiene vocabulario avanzado.	0	1	2	3	4
2. Lea con aptitud y con frecuencia.	0	1	2	3	4
3. Usa sintaxis sofisticada (i.e., la manera de organizar las palabras).	0	1	2	3	4
4. Le gusta hablar de ideas o sentimientos producidos por lo que ha leído o por lo que le hayan leído.	0	1	2	3	4
5. Prefiere libros de niveles avanzados; le gusta la lectura difícil.	0	1	2	3	4
6. Explica precisa y claramente.	0	1	2	3	4
7. Lee o habla con expresión para crear sentido.	0	1	2	3	4
8. Usa el elnguaje de maneras nuevas o poco usuales.	0	1	2	3	4
9. Lee críticamente (i.e., lee con juicio y evaluación).	0	1	2	3	4
10. Usa temas y vocabulario maduro.	0	1	2	3	4
11. Puede buscar muchas maneras de expresar sus ideas para que le entiendan otros.	0	1	2	3	4
12. Puede discutir sobre la literatura u otros temas a un nivel interpretativo (explicativo).	0	1	2	3	4

TOTAL: ☐ = 0 + ___ + ___ + ___ + ___

Escala 3: Matemáticas

1. Reconoce normas y relaciones matemáticas (e.j., extender una secuencia de números; analizar la relación entre dos números).	0	1	2	3	4
2. Aplica ideas de un problema matemático a otro.	0	1	2	3	4
3. Es persistente para encontrar la solución de problemas matemáticos.	0	1	2	3	4
4. Comprende principios matemáticos rápidamente.	0	1	2	3	4
5. Distine rápidamente entre información pertinente y no pertinente en problemas matemáticos.	0	1	2	3	4
6. Usa estrategias creativas y pocos usuales para resolver problemas matemáticos.	0	1	2	3	4
7. Tiene éxito con conceptos matemáticos de niveles avanzados.	0	1	2	3	4
8. Desarrolla múltiples estrategias para resolver problemas matemáticos.	0	1	2	3	4
9. Usa lenguaje matemático correcto.	0	1	2	3	4
10. Tiene conocimiento de una variedad de temas matemáticos.	0	1	2	3	4
11. Se orienta hacia el descubrimiento (i.e., le gusta buscar respuestas a problemas matemáticos.	0	1	2	3	4
12. Sabe la respuesta de muchos problemas por intuición.	0	1	2	3	4

TOTAL: ☐ = 0 + ___ + ___ + ___ + ___

Appendix C: SIGS Home Rating Scales—Spanish, continued

Escala 4: Ciencia

	Nunca	Rara Vez	Igual	Algo Más	Mucho Más
1. Le gusta investigar y explorar temas relacionados con la ciencia.	0	1	2	3	4
2. Puede formular buenas hipótesis basadas en evidencia.	0	1	2	3	4
3. Comprende el proceso científico.	0	1	2	3	4
4. hace preguntas analíticas (i.e., preguntas sobre los elementos de o partes de un problema).	0	1	2	3	4
5. Inicia investigaciones científicas por su cuenta.	0	1	2	3	4
6. Es observador/a; ve detalles.	0	1	2	3	4
7. Puede aplicar un descubrimiento científico de una situación a otra.	0	1	2	3	4
8. Es eficaz en el razonamiento deductivo (i.e., puede comenzar con la idea grande y separarla en partes).	0	1	2	3	4
9. Puede comprender rápidamente relaciones de causa y efecto.	0	1	2	3	4
10. Observa eventos cuidadosamente.	0	1	2	3	4
11. Comprende la relación entre eventos científicos.	0	1	2	3	4
12. Es persistente en llevar a cabo investigaciones científicas.	0	1	2	3	4

TOTAL: ☐ = 0 + __ + __ + __ + __

Escala 5: Estudios Sociales

	Nunca	Rara Vez	Igual	Algo Más	Mucho Más
1. Tiene mucha curiosidad del mundo y eventos de actualidad.	0	1	2	3	4
2. Basa sus opiniones en el bien y el mal.	0	1	2	3	4
3. Le gustan libros de acontecimientos reales de temas sociales.	0	1	2	3	4
4. Hace conexiones entre el pasado y el presente.	0	1	2	3	4
5. Aprecia las diferencias entre culturas mundiales.	0	1	2	3	4
6. Reconoce cómo se relacionan las culturas (e.j., individual a familia gobierno a sociedad).	0	1	2	3	4
7. Busca comprender por qué gente, culturas, o grupos se comportan como lo hacen.	0	1	2	3	4
8. Es apasionado por un período histórico en particular (e.j., las Cruzadas, la Guerra Civil).	0	1	2	3	4
9. Comprende la importancia de usar fuentes que son dignos de confianza.	0	1	2	3	4
10. Desea desarrollar soluciones a problemas sociales.	0	1	2	3	4
11. Busca comprender temas desde muchos puntos de vista.	0	1	2	3	4
12. Tiene un entendimiento de cómo el medio ambiente afecta el estilo de vida de personas.	0	1	2	3	4

TOTAL: ☐ = 0 + __ + __ + __ + __

Escala 6: Creatividad

	Nunca	Rara Vez	Igual	Algo Más	Mucho Más
1. Busca crear en vez de imitar.	0	1	2	3	4
2. Es persistente para encontrar soluciones a problemas.	0	1	2	3	4
3. Es competente para encontrar problemas.	0	1	2	3	4
4. Le gusta tomar riesgos (e.j., no se preocupa por las consecuencias de ser distinto/a ni tiene miedo de cosas nuevas.	0	1	2	3	4
5. Rompe los estereotipos de sexo.	0	1	2	3	4
6. No le importa la incertidumbre.	0	1	2	3	4
7. Le gusta estar solo/a (sobre todo cuando se ocupa en el proceso creativo).	0	1	2	3	4
8. Es excelente para improvisar.	0	1	2	3	4
9. Tiene un talento o interés apasionado (e.j., el arte, la poesía, el escribir, o la ciencia).	0	1	2	3	4
10. Le atrae lo complejo y único.	0	1	2	3	4
11. Le gusta la aventura; está lleno/a de energía.	0	1	2	3	4
12. Valora su propia creatividad.	0	1	2	3	4

TOTAL: ☐ = 0 + __ + __ + __ + __

Appendix C: SIGS Home Rating Scales—Spanish, continued

Escala 7: Liderazgo

	Nunca	Rara Vez	Igual	Algo Más	Mucho Más
1. Sus compañeros lo/la busca para consejos, compañerismo, e ideas.	0	1	2	3	4
2. Es sensible a las necesidades y preocupaciones de otros.	0	1	2	3	4
3. Se adapta fácilmente a nuevas situaciones.	0	1	2	3	4
4. Sus compañeros lo/la considera un/a "pacificador/a."	0	1	2	3	4
5. Tiene disciplina propia.	0	1	2	3	4
6. Tiene un nivel avanzado del entendimiento ético y moral (i.e., reconoce el bien y el mal).	0	1	2	3	4
7. Tiene metas.	0	1	2	3	4
8. Inspira lealtad en otros.	0	1	2	3	4
9. Apoya a sus compañeros.	0	1	2	3	4
10. Es visto/a como una persona justa y atenta.	0	1	2	3	4
11. Tiene altos ideales.	0	1	2	3	4
12. Expresa preocupación e interés por la comunidad y cuestiones del mundo.	0	1	2	3	4

TOTAL: [   ] = 0 + __ + __ + __ + __ __

Summary of Scores:

	Raw Score	Standard Score	Percentile Rank
General Intellectual Ability	[ ]	[ ]	[ ]
Language Arts	[ ]	[ ]	[ ]
Mathematics	[ ]	[ ]	[ ]
Science	[ ]	[ ]	[ ]
Social Studies	[ ]	[ ]	[ ]
Creativity	[ ]	[ ]	[ ]
Leadership	[ ]	[ ]	[ ]

Abedi, J. (2004). Challenges in the No Child Left Behind Act for English-language learners. *Phi Delta Kappan, 85*(10), 782–785 .

Aguirre, N. (2003). ESL students in gifted education. In J. A. Castellano (Ed.), *Special populations in gifted education: Working with diverse gifted learners* (pp. 17–27). Boston: Allyn & Bacon.

Ashman, S. S., & Vukelich, C. (1983). The effect of different types of nomination forms on teachers' identification of gifted children. *Psychology in the Schools, 20*, 518–527.

Baker, C. (2000). *A parents' and teachers' guide to bilingualism* (2nd ed.). Clevedon, England: Multilingual Matters.

Baker, C. (2001). *Foundations of bilingual education and bilingualism* (3rd ed.). Clevedon, England: Multilingual Matters.

Baker, C., & Hornberger, N. H. (Eds.). (2001). *An introductory reader to the writings of Jim Cummins.* Clevedon, England: Multilingual Matters.

Banks, J. A. (1995). Multicultural education: Historical development, dimensions, and practice. In J. A. Banks & C. A. M. Banks (Eds.), *Handbook of research on multicultural education* (pp. 3–24). New York: Macmillan.

Besnoy, K. (2005). Using public relations strategies to advocate for gifted programming in your school. *Gifted Child Today, 28*, 32–37, 65.

Betts, J. R., Zau, A. C., & Rice, L. A. (2003). *New insights into school and classroom factors affecting student achievement.* San Francisco, CA: Public Policy Institute of California.

Bialystok, E. (1991). *Language processing in bilingual children.* New York: Cambridge University Press.

Bracken, B. A., & Brown, E. F. (2004, November). *Behavioral identification of gifted and talented students.* Paper presented at the 51st Annual Convention of the National Association for Gifted Children, Salt Lake City, UT.

Brown, L., Sherbenou, R., & Johnsen, S. K. (1997). *Test of Nonverbal Intelligence* (TONI-3). Austin, TX: Pro-Ed.

Castellano, J. A. (Ed.). (2003). *Special populations in gifted education: Working with diverse gifted learners.* Boston: Allyn & Bacon.

Castellano, J. A. & Díaz, E. (2002). *Reaching new horizons: Gifted and talented education for culturally and linguistically diverse students.* Boston: Allyn & Bacon.

Cummins, J. (1999). *Basic interpersonal communicative skills and cognitive academic language proficiency.* Retrieved January 27, 2005, from http://www.iteachilearn.com/cummins/bic-scalp.html

Dicker, S. J. (2000). Official English and bilingual education: The controversy over language pluralism in U.S. society. In J. K. Hall & W. G. Eggington (Eds.), *The sociopolitics of English language teaching.* Clevedon, England: Multilingual Matters.

Echevarria, J., Vogt, M. E., & Short, D. J. (2004). *Making content comprehensible to English learners: The SIOP model* (2nd ed.). Boston: Allyn & Bacon.

Education of All Handicapped Children Act of 1975, Pub. Law 94-142 (November 29, 1975).

Feuerstein, R., Rand, Y., & Hoffman, M. B. (1979). *The dynamic testing of retarded performers: The learning potential assessment device: Theory, instruments, and techniques.* Baltimore: University Park Press.

Ford, D. Y., & Harris, J. J., III. (1999). *Multicultural gifted education*. New York: Teachers College Press.

Ford, D. Y., Moore, J. L., III, & Milner, H. R. (2005). Beyond culture blindness: A model of culture with implications for gifted education. *Roeper Review, 27*, 97–103.

Frasier, M. M. (1989). Identification of gifted Black students: Developing new perspectives. In C. J. Maker & S. W. Schiever (Eds.), *Critical issues in gifted education: Defensible programs for cultural and ethnic minorities* (Vol. 2, pp. 213–225). Austin, TX: Pro-Ed.

Freedle, R. O. (2002). Correcting the SAT's ethnic and social-class bias: A method for re-estimating SAT scores. *Harvard Educational Review, 72*, 1–43.

Gay, G. (2000). *Culturally responsive teaching: Theory, research, and practice*. New York: Teachers College Press.

Gibbs, W. W. (2002, August). Saving dying languages. *Scientific American, 287*, 78–85.

Golden, D. (2004, April 7). Boosting minorities in gifted programs poses dilemmas; Nontraditional criteria lift admissions of blacks, poor; Fear of diluting programs; New focus on the very top. *Wall Street Journal*, p. 1A.

Gonzalez, V. (Ed.). (1999). *Language and cognitive development in second language learning: Educational implications for children and adults*. Boston: Allyn & Bacon.

Granada, J. (2003). Casting a wider net: Linking bilingual and gifted education. In J. A. Castellano (Ed.), *Special populations in gifted education: Working with diverse gifted learners* (pp. 1–16). Boston: Allyn & Bacon.

Howard, G. R. (1999). *We can't teach what we don't know: White teachers, multiracial schools*. New York: Teachers College Press.

Individuals With Disabilities Education Act, 20 U. S. C. § 1401 et seq. (1990).

Jarosewich, T., Pfeiffer, S. I., & Morris, J. (2002). Identifying gifted students using teacher rating scales: A review of existing instruments. *Journal of Psychoeducational Assessment, 20*, 322–336.

Joint Committee on Standards for Educational and

Psychological Testing of the American Educational Research Association, the American Psychological Association, and the National Council on Measurement in Education. (1999). *Standards for educational and psychological testing.* Washington, DC: Author.

Klein, S., Burgarin, R., Beltranena, R., & McArthur, E. (2004). *Language minorities and their educational and labor market indicators—recent trends* (National Center for Education Statistics Report No. 2004009). Washington, DC: US Department of Education.

Kulik, J. A., & Kulik, C-L. C. (1992). Meta-analytic findings on grouping programs. *Gifted Child Quarterly, 36,* 73–77.

Lessow-Hurley, J. (2003). *Meeting the needs of second language learners: An educator's guide.* Alexandria, VA: Association for Supervision and Curriculum Development.

Lidz, C. S., & Elliott, J. (Eds.). (2000). *Dynamic assessment: Prevailing models and applications.* New York: Elsevier.

Lohman, D. F. (2005a). Review of Naglieri and Ford (2003): Does the Naglieri Nonverbal Ability Test identify equal proportions of high-scoring White, Black, and Hispanic students? *Gifted Child Quarterly, 49,* 19–28.

Lohman, D. F. (2005b). The role of nonverbal ability tests in identifying academically gifted students: An aptitude perspective. *Gifted Child Quarterly, 49,* 111–138.

Martorell, M. (2000). Bilingualism and creativity. In G. B. Esquivel & J. C. Houtz (Eds.), *Creativity and giftedness in culturally diverse students* (pp. 83–101). Cresskill, NJ: Hampton Press.

Matthews, M. S. (2001, April). *Southeastern public education responds to change in Hispanic population, 1985–2000.* Paper presented at the 82nd Annual Meeting of the American Educational Research Association, Seattle, WA. (ERIC document reproduction service No. ED453305)

Matthews, M. S. (2002a). Dynamic assessment of academic ability of bilingual immigrant Latino children. (Doctoral dissertation, University of Georgia, 2002). *Dissertation Abstracts International* 63(02), 498.

Matthews, M. S. (2002b). Parental bilingualism's relationship to creativity of parents and their children. *Gifted and Talented International, 17,* 31–38.

Matthews, M. S. (in press). Gifted students dropping out: New evidence from a Southeastern state. *Roeper Review.*

Matthews, P. H., & Matthews, M. S. (2004). Heritage language instruction and giftedness in language minority students: Pathways toward success. *Journal of Secondary Gifted Education, 15,* 50–55.

Naglieri, J. A. (1996). *Naglieri Nonverbal Ability Test.* San Antonio, TX: Harcourt Brace.

Naglieri, J. A., & Ford, D. Y. (2005). Increasing minority children's participation in gifted classes using the NNAT: A response to Lohman. *Gifted Child Quarterly, 49,* 29–36.

No Child Left Behind Act, 20 U. S. C. § 6301 (2001).

Noel, J. (2000). *Developing multicultural educators.* New York: Longman.

Piper, T. (2003). *Language and learning: The home and school years* (3rd ed.). Upper Saddle River, NJ: Merrill.

Raven, J., Raven, J. C., & Court, J. H. (2000). *Standard Progressive Matrices: Including the parallel and plus versions.* Oxford, UK: Oxford Psychological Press.

Renzulli, J. S., & Park, S. (2002). *Giftedness and high school dropouts: Personal, family, and school-related factors* (Research Monograph No. RM02168). Storrs, CT: The National Research Center on the Gifted and Talented, University of Connecticut.

Renzulli, J. S., Smith, L. H., White, A. J., Callahan, C. M., Hartman, R. K., Westberg, K. L., et al. (2002). *Scales for Rating the Behavioral Characteristics of Superior Students* (Revised ed.). Mansfield Center, CT: Creative Learning Press.

Rimm, S. B., & Lovance, K. J. (1992). The use of subject and grade skipping for the prevention and reversal of underachievement. *Gifted Child Quarterly, 36,* 100–105.

Rivera, C., & Stansfield, C. W. (2004). *Leveling the playing field for English language learners: Increasing participation in state and local assessments through accommodations: Test preparation as an accommodation.* Retrieved September 30, 2005, from

http://www.helpforschools.com/ELLKBase/tips/TestPrepa
sAccommodation.shtml

Rogers, K. B. (2002). *Re-forming gifted education: Matching the program to the child.* Scottsdale, AZ: Great Potential Press.

Ryser, G. R. & McConnell, K. (2004). *Scales for identifying gifted students (SIGS).* Waco, TX: Prufrock Press.

Schmid, C. L. (2001). Educational achievement, language-minority students, and the new second generation. *Sociology of Education, 74,* 71–87.

Siegle, D. (2001, April). *Teacher bias in identifying gifted and talented students.* Paper presented at the 80th Annual Meeting of the Council for Exceptional Children, Kansas City, MO. (ERIC Document Reproduction Service No. ED454664)

Skutnabb-Kangas, T. (2000). Linguistic human rights and teachers of English. In J. K. Hall & W. G. Eggington (Eds.), *The sociopolitics of English language teaching* (pp. 22–44). Clevedon, England: Multilingual Matters.

Smutny, J. F., Walker, S. Y., & Meckstroth, E. A. (1997). *Teaching young gifted children in the regular classroom: Identifying, nurturing, and challenging ages 4–9.* Minneapolis, MN: Free Spirit Publishing.

Sternberg, R. J. (2004). Good intentions, bad results: A dozen reasons why the No Child Left Behind Act is failing our schools. *Education Week, 24*(9), 42, 56.

Sternberg, R. J., & Grigorenko, E. L. (2002). *Dynamic testing: The nature and measurement of learning potential.* New York: Cambridge University Press.

Sternberg, R. J., Grigorenko, E. L., & Bundy, D. A. (2001). The predictive value of IQ. *Merrill-Palmer Quarterly, 47,* 1–41.

Swanson, H. L. (1996). *Swanson-Cognitive Processing Test.* Austin, TX: Pro-Ed.

Swanson, H. L. & Lussier, C. M. (2001). A selective synthesis of the experimental literature on dynamic assessment. *Review of Educational Research 71,* 321–363.

Tokuhama-Espinosa, T. (2001). *Raising multilingual children: Foreign language acquisition and children.* Westport, CT: Bergin & Garvey.

Torrance, E. P., Goff, K., & Satterfield, N. B. (1998). *Multicultural mentoring of the gifted and talented.* Waco, TX: Prufrock Press.

Tzuriel, D. (2001). *Dynamic assessment of young children.* New York: Springer.

UNESCO. (1996). *Universal declaration of linguistic rights.* Retrieved September 29, 2005, from http://www.unesco. org/most/lnngo11.htm

Valdés, G. (Ed.). (2003). *Expanding definitions of giftedness: The case of young interpreters from immigrant communities.* Mahwah, NJ: Lawrence Erlbaum Associates.

Valenzuela, A. (1999). *Subtractive schooling: U.S. Mexican youth and the politics of caring.* Albany: State University of New York Press.

VanTassel-Baska, J. (2003, March 7). *Quo vadis, gifted education?* Paper presented at the Fireside Chat, National Curriculum Network Conference, 15th Year Celebration of the Center for Gifted Education. Retrieved February 22, 2005, from http://cfge.wm.edu/VanTassel-BaskaNCNCSpeech2003.pdf

Wright, W. E. (2005). *Evolution of Federal policy and implications of No Child Left Behind for language minority students.* Tempe, AZ: Education Policy Studies Laboratory, Language Policy Research Unit. Retrieved February 11, 2005, from http://www.asu.edu/educ/epsl/EPRU/documents/EPSL-0501-101-LPRU.pdf

Dr. Michael S. Matthews is an assistant professor in the gifted education program in the Department of Special Education at the University of South Florida in Tampa. Dr. Matthews holds a Ph.D. in educational psychology, with a concentration in gifted and creative education, from the University of Georgia. Prior to moving to USF, he was a postdoctoral Research Fellow at the Duke University Talent Identification Program.

Dr. Matthews is a regular presenter at state, national, and international meetings on gifted education. He is also the 2006 Program Chair for the special interest group, Research on Giftedness and Talent, of the American Educational Research Association. He serves as a reviewer for journals that include *Gifted Child Quarterly*, *Journal of Secondary Gifted Education*, and *Journal for the Education of the Gifted*. At the University of South Florida, Dr. Matthews teaches graduate classes on giftedness and creativity. His research interests include underachievement, science education, and varied issues related to cultural and linguistic diversity in gifted education.